GRAMERCY GREAT MASTERS

Acknowledgments

The publishers would like to thank the museums for reproduction permission and in particular the **BRIDGEMAN ART LIBRARY** and **SCALA Istituto Fotografico Editoriale** for their help in supplying the illustrations for the book.

Art Institute of Chigago: The Beach at Sainte-Adresse.

Boston Museum of Fine Arts, Massachusetts: Madame Monet in Japanese Costume ("La Japonaise"); Poppy Field near Giverny.

Cleveland Museum of Art: Bazille and Camille: Study for Le Déjeuner sur l'herbe.

Christie's, London: The Seine at Chatou near Argenteuil; The Banks of the River Epte at Giverny; Springtime at Giverny; Rouen Cathedral, Early Morning; Water Lilies.

Galerie Bayeler: Water Lilies.

Glasgow Art Gallery & Museum: View Towards Ventimiglia.

Kunsthalle, Bremen: Woman in a Green Dress (Camille).

Louvre: The Luncheon; The Railway Bridge at Argenteuil; The Bridge of Argenteuil.

Mellon Bruce, Washington: Spring Flowers.

Metropolitan Museum of Art, New York: The Terrace at Sainte-Adresse.

Minneapolis Society of Fine Arts: The Japanese Footbridge, Giverny.

Museu de Arte de São Paulo, Brazil: Boating on the River Epte.

Musée de Grenoble: The Garden at Giverny.

Musée de L'Orangerie, Paris: Red Boats, Argenteuil.

Musée des Beaux Arts, Rouen: Rue Saint-Denis, Celebration of June 30, 1878.

Musée d'Orsay, Paris: The Tulip Field; Women in the Garden; The Hotel Roches Noires, Trouville; Meditation: Madame Monet on a Sofa; The Magpie; A Field of Poppies; Chrysanthemums; The Gare St. Lazare; Lady with a Parasol; Storm at Belle-Isle; Grain Stacks at the End of Summer; Rouen Cathedral: Harmony in Blue and Gold, Full Sunlight; The Water Lily Pond: Harmony in Rose; The Houses of Parliament, London: the Sun Breaking through Fog.

Musée Marmottan, Paris: Impression: Sunrise; Train in the Snow.

National Gallery, London: Bathers at La Grenouillère; Lavacourt under Snow.

National Gallery of Art, Washington: The Artist's Garden at Vétheuil.

National Museum of Wales, Cardiff: View of San Giorgio Maggiore, Venice.

Palace of the Legion of Honor, San Francisco: The Grand Canal, Venice.

Pushkin Museum, Moscow: The Picnic ("Le Déjeuner sur l'herbe"); The Boulevard des Capucines; Rouen Cathedral, Evening.

Private Collection: The Bridge at Bougival.

Published by Gramercy Books
distributed by Random House Value Publishing, Inc.
40 Engelhard Avenue
Avenel, New Jersey 07001

Printed and bound in Italy

ISBN: 0-517-12402-5

10 9 8 7 6 5 4 3 2 1

Claude Monet

GRAMERCY BOOKS

NEW YORK • AVENEL

Claude Monet
His Life and Works

Born in Paris in November 1840, Monet lived for more than eighty-five years, his life spanning a period that saw momentous social and political events on the European scene. These events, necessarily, had an effect on the life and work of this sensitive and attentive artist. One need only think of the difficult relations between the Impressionists and the art market in the period between the Second Empire and the Third Republic to understand that Monet — like Manet, Pissarro and all the others who formed part of that circle of uncompromising rebels against the established canons of art — had to fight on various fronts. Indeed, as his artistic career unfolded, from his early caricatures to the discovery of outdoor painting, and then on to the final extraordinary achievement of *Water Lilies*, this reserved and solitary man was forced to spend most of his life fighting. He fought against lack of interest on the part of the critics, faced hostility from the official painters of the Salon des Beaux-Arts and suffered ridicule from a public that preferred obsessively precise portraits of prominent personalities to a new vision of reality.

Ironically enough, this new trend was, however, finally accepted. Indeed, Monet became the symbol in art of that same bourgeois class that had previously so opposed it. The bourgeoisie was the obvious target audience of the Impressionists, for they saw it as embodying the new and free society that had risen out of the ashes of the *ancien régime*. As it turned out, this "radical renovation," the goal sought by many intellectuals of the time, failed to take place. As Émile Zola coldly observed, when society began to accept these new works, it was only under the guidance and with the reassurance of the academic juries and official criticism.

None of this, however, detracts from the greatness of the Impressionists — nor in particular from Monet, who was considered

Windmills near Zaandam
(detail)

the movement's leading exponent. Scandal as a means of awakening people to new consciousness was less important to him than painting landscapes in the fullest possible light, thereby creating something precious to offer to the world. With a study of Claude Monet, we approach the very heart of the Impressionist enterprise. This humble painter, who grew up in Le Havre and was taught by Jongkind and Boudin to contemplate vast natural landscapes and to observe the variations in light between expanses of water and clear, blue skies, was the man who produced the most mature, and the most exciting and innovative, outdoor paintings.

EARLY CAREER

Born in Rue Lafitte in Paris on November 14, 1840, Claude Oscar Monet spent his early childhood in the port of Le Havre, where his father, a grocer by trade, had been forced to move to improve his business prospects. Here, at the mouth of the Seine, Monet made his first excursions into the figurative arts under the guidance of François Charles Ochard, a disciple of David. His landscapes and numerous caricatures from around 1856 showed evidence of great technical skill in the use of pencil and charcoals. His precocious ability brought him to the notice of Eugène Boudin, a painter who owned a framemaker's shop in Le Havre.

Boudin gave the young painter the chance to display his paintings in his shop window, thus helping Monet to gain a certain degree of local fame. Boudin was himself a genuine landscape artist and he initiated Monet into the technique of outdoor painting. At first, Monet was not totally convinced by Boudin's conception of painting; but later he began to appreciate that this marine painter was probably right to suggest, as he often did, that Monet give up drawing caricatures and devote himself entirely to painting. Thus, in May 1854, armed with a letter of introduction to Troyon, a long-standing member of the school of Barbizon, and with his father's permission, he set off for Paris.

Once there, Monet, who was already hostile to academic authority, ignored Troyon's advice, deciding instead to attend lessons at the Académie Suisse. This was an unofficial academy where the fees were reasonable and where Monet knew he could also work with live models. It was while attending this "free academy" that he became friends with Camille Pissarro, who was ten years his elder. Together, they started to frequent the Brasserie des Martyrs, a meeting place for the group of realist painters headed by Courbet. Again, accompanied by Pissarro but this time with an easel on his back, Monet began to explore the countryside around Paris, complementing his studio education with the experience of the open air that he had already started to enjoy under Boudin's guidance.

In 1861 military service took him to Algeria, and like Delacroix before him in 1832, he was deeply impressed by the vivid colors and intensity of light of the North African landscape. A year later, on sick leave in Le Havre, he once again took up painting with his old friend Boudin. Together with an accomplished Dutch painter named Jongkind, the three of them spent much of the summer painting in the open air. It was an experience that, as Monet himself was to observe, went a long way in helping him perfect his technique. He had an eye that observed lovingly and joyfully the thousands of small marvels that make up the diversity of nature. He was a visual poet, able to translate his impressions onto the canvas while at the same time keeping their freshness of feeling intact.

THE STUDIO OF GLEYRE

At the end of 1862, Monet's father, concerned about his son's delicate health, decided to free him from his military obligations, and Monet returned to Paris, where he began to pay regular visits to the studio of Gleyre. Gleyre was a capable Swiss painter who, more for his generosity than for his ideological convictions, had gained a liberal reputation, and his school attracted young talents who had no time for the official procedures of the École des Beaux-Arts. Other pupils of Gleyre's at that time included Renoir, Sisley and Bazille. It was his friendship with these artists that proved more useful to Monet than Gleyre's teaching.

With these new companions, Monet was able to satisfy his taste for outdoor painting, taking his easel out into the beautiful forest of Fontainebleau. These excursions, with the first group of painters who were to become the Impressionists, confirmed Monet's technical supremacy over most of his younger colleagues, a supremacy acquired through his work with Boudin and Jongkind.

In this period, the artist began to realize that it was time to throw off the role of disciple that he had assumed in relation to other painters in his circle. It was perhaps for this reason that Monet abandoned work on *Déjeuner sur l'herbe*. The title of the painting marked it as a clear homage to Manet, while in style it reflected in many ways the influence of Courbet. He began instead to devote himself to the portrait *Camille*. This painting was accepted by the official Salon in 1866 and secured him a certain degree of success. The figure in green in the portrait was Camille Doncieux, his companion and model, a lovely young lady who was to give birth to his two sons, Jean and Michel, before dying of illness at the early age of thirty-two. On that same occasion the Salon accepted another of Monet's works which at the time aroused less interest but was later to prove crucial in any study of his artistic development: *St.- Germain l'Auxerrois*, painted from a balcony of the Louvre. The painting focuses upon the way the dazzling light falls on the leaves of the trees, blending with the green of the lawns and the gray of the houses in a manner that is decidedly impressionistic.

OFFICIAL INCOMPREHENSION

At this point in his career Monet began to have doubts about his artistic progress thus far. The controversy surrounding the Salon des Refusés showed him the limitations of the debate that was taking place between an intolerant tradition on the one hand and romantic aspirations on the other. The Salon des Refusés had been set up by Napoleon III in 1863; this was the year the academic Salon refused to accept almost four thousand of the works submitted, provoking a veritable uprising among the artists. The Emperor reacted by ordering that the rejected works be housed in premises next door to the official Salon. The parallel exhibition was, however, to prove a fiasco and a scandal. The days when conventional painters would adopt the bright palette of the Impressionists were still a long way off.

Although Monet himself did not participate in the Salon des Refusés, he could certainly not be accused of fawning over the Academy. Despite the acceptance of *Camille* and (in subsequent years) of other works, his relations with the official market remained difficult for quite some time. This had negative consequences on the spread of his art as well as on his financial state.

Monet's landscapes are undoubtedly among his highest artistic achievements, but his human figures are also seen in a limpid atmospheric relationship, as demonstrated by the fragment and sketch that are all that remain of his lost masterpiece *Déjeuner sur l'herbe*. Even in its fragmentary form, it preserves all the enchantment of extraordinary freshness with its stark contrast between grays and vivid reds.

The 1866 work *Women in the Garden* marks another stage in Monet's development. Although it follows a precise pattern, with its well-defined but stylized profiles and planes, this large-scale painting, executed completely outdoors, already shows signs of remarkable artistic boldness — which was probably the reason for its rejection by the Salon the following year. The scene shows some female figures in a bourgeois garden on the outskirts of Paris. Camille Doncieux herself posed for three of these figures, all intent on picking and smelling flowers. The chances of such an everyday scene interesting the Salon were in themselves remote, but the jury's decision to reject the painting was probably due less to the subject than to the presence of extreme contrasts in light and the use of vivid colors. The painting was purchased by Bazille, another member of the group, whose financial position — he was the son of a senator — allowed him to help out those of his colleagues who were in difficulty. Like many other Impressionists, Monet certainly did not lead a life of ease. This was especially true after his father, who disapproved not so much of his son's passion for painting as his rebellious attitude, cut off all assistance in 1864.

In 1867, Monet's activity became truly large-scale: he was working on a total of twenty paintings in which figures, gardens, views of Le Havre and scenes of regattas flowed freely on the canvas, reflecting his continuing interest in the tonality of light and the question of how to capture the play of changing light. In the autumn of the same year, immediately after the birth of his first son, Jean, he moved to Paris together with Bazille and Renoir. His friendship with Renoir was almost that of artistic brotherhood, and the two continued to work side by side as they had during their first exercises in outdoor painting at Fontainebleau.

LA GRENOUILLERE
The following year, the painter started to paint his "views from the riverside," a theme that was to take on such great importance in the formation of the Impressionist style. This was not so much because of the motif itself, as because of the opportunity it offered

The Floating Studio
(detail)

15

to the painter to make color the constructive element of the painting. This concept was developed in the works dedicated to the Grenouillère, the picturesque landing stage often painted by both Renoir and Monet during the period when they worked together, sharing not only artistic experiences but also a house near Bougival on the Seine.

The work entitled *La Grenouillère* can, in many respects, be considered the first distinctly Impressionist painting. It is a work of great technical audacity, using free play of color and smooth brushstrokes in an attempt to capture the momentary thrill of life itself. There is a sudden burst of green in the leaves as they are struck by the rays of the sun, and dazzling reflections glance off the surface of the water where light and shade weave an intricate pattern.

In 1870, Monet officially married his companion Camille and the couple moved to Normandy. At the outbreak of the Franco-Prussian War, Monet, true to his republican ideas, refused to fight for the Emperor, taking refuge in London. Here he again met his old friend Pissarro and became acquainted with Durand-Ruel, the first art dealer who had sufficient faith in the Impressionists to risk capital in their works. In London, the painter came to know the works of Turner and Constable and was fascinated by their interest in the "colors of nature."

Before returning to France, Monet spent some time in Holland and thus remained largely untouched by political and social events of this period, such as the famous "Paris Commune." In Holland he was fascinated by the serene Dutch landscape with its windmills reflected in the calm waters of the canals. He returned to France with several studies and canvases as well as a large number of Japanese prints that he had bought in Amsterdam. These prints — by Hokusai, Hiroshige and Korin — were to have an influence on his art in the years to come, contributing to the boldness of certain artistic choices, especially in the juxtaposition of colors. By this time, there had been an improvement in Monet's financial position. Camille's dowry and the legacy he received on his father's death enabled him to lead a comfortable life, allowing him also to move with his family to Argenteuil on the Seine, to a house surrounded by a lovely garden where he began to cultivate his passion for flowers.

The Nadar Studio Scandal

In 1873, Monet met the wealthy art collector Caillebotte and a genuine friendship grew between them. Caillebotte, himself a good amateur painter, was to become one of the main champions of Impressionism, organizing many of its exhibitions. Monet at this time was tacitly beginning to take over from Manet the role of leader of the group of Impressionist artists.

The following year, 1874, was to prove a fundamental date in the history of the Impressionists and in the history of art itself. The circle of artists around Monet — which included Manet, Renoir, Pissarro and others — found themselves in dire economic straits. Durand-Ruel, who had purchased many paintings after the Commune, was forced to stop buying their works as his customers did not appreciate them. The Salon jury rejected many of their paintings, leaving the group of innovators with no choice but to organize its own exhibition in order to reach a wide audience. The idea had been in the air since 1870, but was then taken up again and endorsed by Manet, with the warm support of all the others.

There was a risk, however, that it would become another Salon des Refusés; in other words, an exhibition that could be seen as hostile to the world of the Salon and stamped as a collection of rejected works before it got off the ground. Degas made the reasonable suggestion of inviting other painters to participate in the exhibition, painters from outside their group who were already known to both critics and public. Although the proposal met with some negative comment and sparked off arguments among the future Impressionists, it was accepted in the end. However, their precautions had all been taken in vain: the works of the thirty artists exhibited in the studio of the photographer Nadar on April 1874 unleashed a storm of vehement reactions ranging from derision to disgust. Hanging on the velvet-draped walls were masterpieces such as *The Loggia* by Renoir and *The Dance Examination* by Degas. In all, there were 165 paintings, among them *Impression: Sunrise*, a work Monet had painted in Le Havre in 1872, and which, as we shall see, came to give its name to the whole movement.

As such, the exhibition was a disaster, although its publicity value was enormous. The numerous visitors were not inclined to buy the works on display and the few that were sold brought in ridiculously little money. Typically, the critics showed no mercy. One of them,

Snow at Argenteuil
(detail)

18

taking his inspiration from the title of the work referred to above, dubbed Monet and his companions "Impressionists." Strangely, the critic's article on the exhibition, while sarcastic, was not particularly hostile or vulgar and the poor journalist could not have imagined that the butt of his irony was to become one of the most famous movements in the history of art.

Another of Monet's canvases exhibited at Nadar's studio — besides the scandalous *Impression: Sunrise* — was also to become famous. This was *A Field of Poppies*, a small-scale work that depicts a woman and a child (almost certainly the artist's family) in a field, and the same couple repeated in the lower part of the canvas, as if to suggest the idea of movement. It is an exquisite painting, able to conjure up the spontaneity of a sketch, but revealing at the same time an unwavering attention to the rhythm and balance of the whole.

THE INDIVIDUAL QUEST

This period saw Monet starting to free himself from the ties of well-defined artistic movements. As a result, in subsequent years, his character became more and more reserved and solitary, his nature more reflective. Nevertheless, his artistic quest continued. He was fascinated by the idea of painting fog-shrouded landscapes, and for him the bursts of steam given off by departing locomotives were, in Renoir's words, "enchanting, a veritable phantasmagoria." Thus originated the series of works that focuses on stations.

In *The Gare St.-Lazare* (1877), the painter lowers his point of view almost to the level of the railway tracks, and the human figures seem almost to disappear in the swirling whitish-blue smoke. In its execution one can see the first signs of the method that later gave rise to the canvases depicting Rouen Cathedral. The old houses of a Parisian street can be glimpsed through the smoky atmosphere of the station. The painting is dominated by a floral blue cloud, a motif which although repeated in other paintings always arouses the excitement of a fresh discovery.

In 1877 there were two further sales of Impressionist paintings organized, one of which took place at the Hôtel Drouot. The artists belonging to the group had by now accepted the epithet of Impressionists, and they presented themselves as such to the public and the critics. Over the next few years there was a succession of exhibitions, which, independent of the actual commercial and critical success they enjoyed at the time, were important in getting this new art to be accepted by even the most backward academics.

The following year, Camille gave birth to their second son, Michel, and the family's economic difficulties increased. Most of the letters Monet wrote during this period were requests for help, addressed not only to colleagues but also to dealers and collectors. One collector, Hoschedé, became his friend and helped with accommodation for a time, long enough in fact for the painter to fall in love with the collector's wife, Alice.

One of the paintings completed that year, *The Banks of the Seine,* shows how Monet's artistic quest was a never-ending process. It shows the artist experimenting with a new technique, where the brushwork consists of short, nervous commas, which lend an extraordinary vibration to the painting.

In 1879 Monet moved with his family to Vétheuil on the Seine. Although the reasons for the move were economic, Monet found the village, in his own words, "a delightful place." The view it offered — a bend in the river dotted with wooded islets — could not fail to have an effect on someone of Monet's artistic spirit. He painted numerous canvases whose subject is the snow-covered village, and these gave him the opportunity to make a close study of light and reflections. In one, *Vétheuil Church,* the entire canvas is dominated by a massive square bell tower, and the whole composition unfolds vertically, with a horizontal line in the foreground acting as an effective counterbalance. In order to depict the snow-covered riverbank, Monet employed the same fragmentary brushstrokes he had used to suggest the movement of water.

In September 1879, Camille fell victim to her illness. Her place as the painter's companion as well as that of mother to Jean and Michel was taken by Alice Hoschedé, who had sometime previously left her husband's house and moved to be near the Monets, followed later by her children. By this time, Monet's role as the cohesive force binding the various Impressionist artists together was coming to an end. He refused to act as "leader" and isolated himself increasingly. In 1880, he submitted two works to the jury of the Salon, but only one was accepted. It was to be the last time he was exhibited there. As attracted as ever to outdoor painting and intent on working alone, he rediscovered the fascination of the Normandy coastline, which had previously inspired him when he was painting at Trouville. He visited Fécamp, where the exceptional beauty of the countryside impressed him enormously. He was to return there on numerous occasions, drawn by the mists that lent themselves so readily to his studies in light and the transparency of the air.

THE SPLIT IN THE IMPRESSIONIST MOVEMENT

The definitive split in the Impressionist group took place in April 1881. As we have seen, Monet was already beginning to become detached from the shared aspirations of the group. He now took a more open stand against them, but he still had Cézanne, Renoir and Sisley on his side. Although he never left the group completely, Monet became increasingly isolated, both from the public and in his own work. In 1883, a one-man show with fifty works opened at Durand-Ruel's gallery, while 1886 saw the creation of one of Monet's and Impressionism's most famous works: *Woman with Parasol Turned Towards the Left* — a mirror image of an almost identical painting executed by the painter in that same year. He had painted it at Giverny, a small town at the confluence of the Epte and the Seine rivers. Captivated by the beauty of the place, Monet had decided to move there shortly before, and it was there that he was to spend the remaining thirty-five years of his life.

By this time, Monet had long given up his studies of the human figure; but in 1886, for one last time, he turned again to the subject that had occupied him at the beginning of his career. Very probably the model for this work was Suzanne, Alice's daughter. However this is not certain because Monet was so struck by the fascination of the scene that he only sketched the young girl's face. The movement of the dress and the grass give the impression of a windy day, and there is an extraordinary harmony in the way the figure blends with the clouds in the background: Monet had created a woman out of wind, light and color.

Giverny was an ideal place for painting: the countryside surrounding the village and the constant change in the waters of the Seine gave him a stream of ideas, and the garden of the small rented cottage which he cultivated lovingly was already becoming a true source of inspiration. Nevertheless, the painter agreed to go with Renoir on a journey to the Italian Riviera. He was then so struck by the beauty of the place that he decided to rent a house at

Rouen Cathedral
(detail)

Bordighera for some months. When he returned to France he brought with him more than fifty canvases, half of which were sketches or studies.

HAYSTACKS, POPLARS AND CATHEDRALS

The period around 1883 was not an easy one for Monet. He was concerned about the crisis in his relationship with Alice and beyond that, about the general crisis in the art market. The artist's reaction to this latter problem was to seek to spread his reputation, which was on the point of becoming fame in the true sense of the word.

He took part in an Impressionist exhibition held in New York organized by Durand-Ruel. He exhibited with the "Vingt" group in Brussels, a city that was rapidly becoming the new hub of the art market. In the period up to 1889 he participated on several occasions at Georges Petit's International Exhibitions, further reinforcing his increasing fame. In 1888, after his contract with Durand-Ruel had been terminated, he became friends with Vincent van Gogh's brother Theo, who helped him exhibit at the Boussod & Valadon gallery in Paris. His acquaintance with the critics Gustave Geffroy and Octave Mirabeau helped him gain the appreciation of a wider public, although his relations with official critics and the jury of the Salon remained cold. Monet's proud spirit is demonstrated, for example, by his refusal to accept the award of the Légion d'honneur. In 1889 the Petit Gallery held a retrospective of Monet's work consisting of a total of 145 paintings completed between 1864 and 1889. The painter took this occasion to attack the academic world for its groundless hostility, criticizing in the introduction to the catalogue the Salon's behavior toward him and the numerous occasions on which his works had been turned down.

By the following year, Monet was prosperous enough to be able to afford to buy a house with some land in Giverny where he started on the creation of a pond and Japanese-style garden. Soon his studio, as well as the pond with its famous water lilies, became a veritable mecca for artists and art collectors, not only from France but from all over Europe.

Some critics maintain that the improvement in Monet's finances coincided with a certain loss of artistic spontaneity. The fact is, however, that although his treatment of themes became more methodical from 1890 on, this was due not to a lack of inspiration, but rather to the attempt to record the continuous, successive changes in light as it played on the same subject — variations that the changes in luminosity imposed on the subject, modifying it and at the same time modifying the relationship between the artist and the work. It is unfair to depict the mature Monet as an imitator of himself. The fact is that he remained an untiring innovator, ever renewing his own technical and stylistic means. Only in the last year of the century did his way of working start to become fanatically methodical. It must also be remembered that even as young painter, when he used to vary theme and approach frequently, his happy inspirations were always backed up by painstaking preparation, which always took into consideration the time of day and the size of the canvas.

Over a period of several years, starting from 1892, Monet produced a remarkable series of paintings, mainly of haystacks, poplars and cathedrals. In these works, the subject is analyzed and taken up an infinite number of times, at different times of day and from varying angles, with highly sophisticated and complex results. The series "Cathedrals of Rouen" is perhaps the most renowned from this period. Monet started these paintings between February and April 1892, and after months of concentrated work he had completed twenty canvases. If we consider three of these paintings in succession — *Early in the Morning; Harmony in Blue and Gold, Full Sunlight;* and *In the Evening* — we can see the metamorphosis of the subject. The first painting is dominated by white and gray light and shows the cathedral set back a little, while in the full sunlight of the second painting it appears much larger and more massive. In the evening, the building gives the impression of having fallen behind its façade, a feeling that is reinforced by the evanescence of the spires.

Even while engaged on these important works Monet still continued his habit of traveling widely. In addition to his frequent trips to different parts of France, he also visited and worked in London in 1891 and Norway in 1895, where he was fascinated by the fjords and the cold beauty of the landscape.

In 1897, the important Caillebotte collection passed to the National Museums, and some Impressionist masterpieces finally made their way into the state collection. Yet only thirty-eight out

Turkeys
(detail)

of sixty-seven paintings donated were accepted. Clearly, the artistic establishment was still not enthusiastic about the works of Renoir, Monet and other major Impressionists.

WATER LILIES "BLOSSOMING IN THE MIDST OF THE SKY"

In June 1898, Monet once again had the great satisfaction of seeing a large one-man show meet with a favorable reception when sixty-one of his works were put on display at the Petit Gallery. However, the following year Monet and his companion suffered a grievous loss with the sudden death of Alice's daughter Suzanne, who had posed for several of Monet's paintings. It was also during this period that his close friend Alfred Sisley passed away. Perhaps in search of distraction from his sorrow, Monet set off for London, where he lived and worked, more or less continuously, for three years. Here he painted his famous views of the Thames; and in 1904, *The Houses of Parliament, London: the Sun Breaking through Fog* which shows Monet still tenaciously continuing his studies of those effects of changes in atmosphere that he had initiated with cathedrals and which increasingly sought to break free from the constraints of merely objective perception. In the autumn of 1899, Monet had also embarked on a cycle of works, "The Water Lilies," which was destined to occupy him for the rest of his life. He continued to work on this project during his stay in London, alternating between it and his views of the Thames, while at the same time acting as curator of his exhibitions, put on by Durand-Ruel. One exhibition, in 1900, contained twenty-six works; another, in 1904, featured his London scenes.

In 1908, at the height of this fruitful period, Monet fell ill, and his eyesight, which had already begun to cause him problems some years earlier, weakened even further. Yet this was not enough to make him stop painting. On the contrary, he moved to Venice and took up work again with great enthusiasm. In particular, the lagoon of Venice inspired him, its light, its structure and its atmosphere corresponding perfectly to his interests. It was during this period that he painted *The Palazzo da Mula in Venice*. The most striking feature of this painting is that half the composition is taken up by water; the beautiful palace, with its arcades and loggias, seems almost to materialize out of the canal waters themselves in the form of gleams and cold reflections.

26

The Water Lily Pond:
Harmony in Rose
(detail)

Despite intermittent journeys in search of other subjects, Monet never really stopped working on the long "Water Lily" cycle, and the results were soon evident: in 1890 the artist had shown about ten *Water Lilies* at the Durand-Ruel gallery, and by 1909 he was able to exhibit forty-eight canvases with this subject. He continued to paint all of these works in his own garden at Giverny. Monet considered the water lilies that grew in the pond to be his "most beautiful masterpiece." The first works were executed outdoors, others from memory in his studio. The whole set of paintings is unique and constitutes a kind of testimony of the passing of time recorded in the movement of light. In remembering the "Water Lilies" series in his *Remembrance of Times Past*, Proust observed that Monet seemed to have made them "blossom in the midst of the sky."

In 1911, Alice died, and was buried in the small graveyard at Giverny. Three years later, her daughter, Blanche Hoschedé, moved in to live with the painter. She helped him in his loneliness, which, now that his first child, Jean, was dead and his second, Michel, had left for the Western Front, was almost total. Yet a further loss befell the now aging master with the death of Auguste Renoir, his last surviving friend from the studio of Gleyre.

Meanwhile, Monet's sight was failing rapidly and his fear of undergoing a cataract operation held him back from remedying this particularly painful situation. In 1922, almost totally blind, Monet was painting desperately in the open air, just one step ahead of the day when the beauty of these color changes which he had spent his entire life trying to capture would be lost to him forever.

The following year, he decided to go ahead with the eye operation, but the benefits were only temporary. He continued to paint in almost total isolation, both outdoors and in his studio, working on enormous wall panels depicting his water lilies. Yet his mood was sad, anxious and discouraged. It was as if his constant need to find ever new ways of investigating the essence of things and their intimate connection with the person painting them prevented him from ever being satisfied with the results he achieved. For some time, as his popularity grew, young artists had started to distance themselves from him; and in a letter to Durand-Ruel written in 1912 he talked of his canvases in the following terms: "I know that if I exhibited them they would be very successful, but none of this matters to me because I am sure that they are ugly."

Self-Portrait

29

*The Palazzo
da Mula, Venice*
(detail)

30

Monet died at his house in Giverny on December 6, 1926. In accordance with his final wishes, the funeral was held without speeches or pomp of any kind. The following year, the panels with his beloved water lilies, his final work, were installed in the Orangerie of the Tuileries in Paris.

BEYOND FORM

If it is true that Monet's work more than any others' merits the term "Impressionist," and Monet himself was seen as the most persistent experimenter in the group, or even its theorist, it is equally true that this painter who was always looking ahead, always in a desperate search for new results, remains in many respects difficult to place as an artist.

Monet is an Impressionist who often went beyond Impressionism, arriving, finally, perhaps not at the total elimination of form, but at its radical redefinition, much as we can find in certain experimental music and poetry. Today, we recognize an extraordinary modernity in his work, as if he had been just a step away from the later art form that became known as "informal."

He himself was perhaps in some way aware of this when he wrote: "I expend my efforts on a maximum of appearances in close correlation with unknown realities." It is remarkable how, despite the hardships of a poor and sad life, Monet's genius always allowed him to draw on nature for impressions that radiate such happiness. Without ever making any concessions to the taste of the time or following the precepts of contemporary critics, Monet continued on his path, for many years fulfilling the role of leader in the group of Impressionists. When the elderly Monet withdrew to his home in Giverny it was to concentrate solely on painting the irises and water lilies in his garden, and this he did with such unprecedented sensibility and stylistic perfection as to become a figure of veneration for all the painters of France.

Spring Flowers

Bathers at La Grenouillère

Bazille and Camille: Study for le Déjeuner sur l'herbe

Bazille and Camille: Study for Le Déjeuner sur l'herbe (detail)

The Terrace at Sainte-Adresse

Women in the Garden

Woman in a Green Dress (Camille)

The Beach at Sainte-Adresse

The Picnic (“Le Déjeuner sur l'herbe”)

The Bridge at Bougival

The Hotel Roches Noires, Trouville

Meditation: Madame Monet on a Sofa

The Luncheon

Impression: Sunrise

The Magpie

The Boulevard des Capucines

A Field of Poppies

The Bridge at Argenteuil

Train in the Snow

The Railway Bridge at Argenteuil

The Seine at Chatou near Argenteuil

Red Boats, Argenteuil

Madame Monet in Japanese Costume ("La Japonaise")

Madame Monet in Japanese Costume ("La Japonaise") (detail)

Chrysanthemums

The Gare St.-Lazare

Rue Saint-Denis, Celebration of June 30, 1878

The Artist's Garden at Vétheuil

Winter Snow

View towards Ventimiglia

The Banks of the River Epte at Giverny

Springtime at Giverny

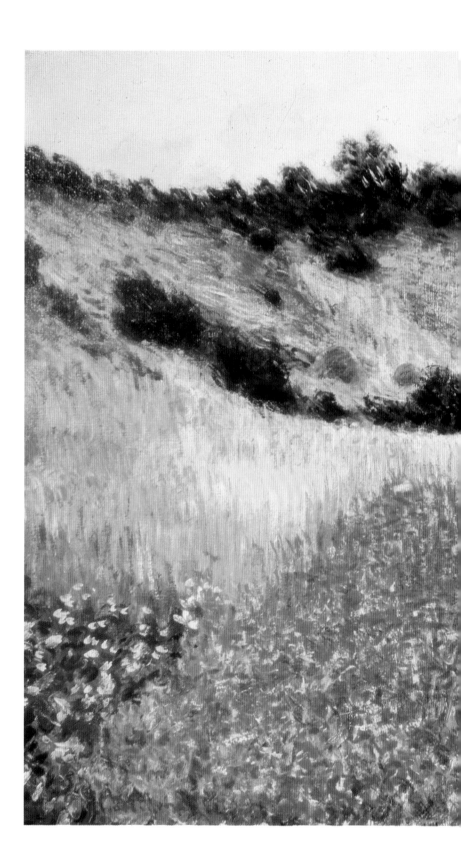

Poppy Field near Giverny

Lady with a Parasol

The Tulip Field

Storm at Belle-Isle

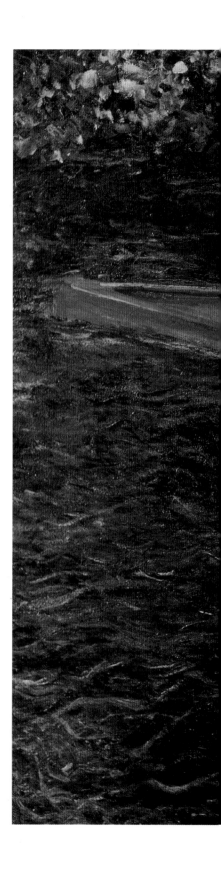

Boating on the River Epte

Grain Stacks at the End of Summer

Rouen Cathedral, Early Morning

Rouen Cathedral: Harmony in Blue and Gold, Full Sunlight

Rouen Cathedral, Evening

Water Lily Pond: Harmony in Rose

Japanese Bridge

The Houses of Parliament, London: the Sun Breaking through Fog

The Grand Canal, Venice

View of San Giorgio Maggiore, Venice

Water Lilies

Water Lilies

The Garden at Giverny